RAPTURED

Matt Lyle
&
Matt Coleman

BROADWAY PLAY PUBLISHING INC
New York
www.broadwayplaypub.com
info@broadwayplaypub.com

RAPTURED
© Copyright 2020 Matt Lyle and Matt Coleman

Cover art by Kim Lyle

First edition: April 2020
I S B N: 978-0-88145-864-0

Book design: Marie Donovan
Page make-up: Adobe InDesign
Typeface: Palatino

RAPTURED was first produced by Theatre Three (Artistic Director, Jeffrey Schmidt; Managing Director, Merri Brewer; Company Manager, Sarah Barnes) in Dallas, opening on 25 April 2019 and closing on 19 May. The cast and creative contributors were:

AL ....Jeff Swearingen
DICK.. Chad Cline
GRACIE..Sally Soldo
MARTHA ....Shannon J McGrann
ROBIN..Jeremy Whiteker
RUTH...Stephanie Cleghorn Jasso
SAM.. Jakie Cabe
TONYA .... Alle Mims
TROY ....Christopher Lew

Director.. Jeffrey Schmidt
Scenic design...David Walsh
Costume design.. Sarah Harris
Lighting design .... Aaron Johansen
Sound design...Marco Salinas
Fight / Intimacy choreography..................Jeffrey Colangelo
Stage manager .... Katie Marchant
Production assistant &
  Props master ....Emily Ann Probus

CHARACTERS & SETTING

SAM, *a smooth talking con man posing as a southern preacher, 30s-50s, M*

AL, SAM's *unwitting sidekick. He believes everything he hears, 20s-40s, M*

GRACIE, *the church's busy body, 60s-70s, F*

MARTHA, *the church's secretary, 30s-40s, F*

ROBIN, *the poorly closeted youth and music pastor for the church, 30s-40s, M*

RUTH, *the church's part-time accountant. Sincere and beloved by everyone, 30s-40s, F*

DICK, RUTH's *no good husband, 30s-40s, M*

TONYA, *a young woman, 19-20, F*

TROY, *a young man, 19-20, M*

All roles can be any ethnicity.

ACT ONE

(Lights up on SAM. *He's on his knees praying and holding an offering plate full of keys.)*

SAM: Dear Lord, if you could find it in your heart this once to help me out of a little bit of a jam I seem to have gotten myself into. I admit I've had a good run here. This place is pretty much heaven for someone like me, but…I have to go now. And I've never asked you for much. I've never asked you to open doors for me, Lord! I've always opened my own doors! But this once, will you please find it in your blessed heart to open this gosh darn door? *(He kicks the door.)* Guide my hand, oh lord…

(The lights have risen fully on the fellowship hall of a church. SAM *picks through an offering plate until he feels compelled by a certain key.)*

SAM: This one lord? Is this the key to my liberation? *(He tries it. It doesn't work.)* Ahh! Look, I know I'm an atheist, Lord, but PLEASE! *(He feverishly starts trying to unlock the center stage door with key after key.)* Mmm— Gah. Okay. No. C'mon. We don't have this many doors! C'mon. No. No.

(The door leading to the chapel opens and GRACIE *enters. You can hear a congregation singing.)*

SAM: Ah!

GRACIE: Brother Sam! There you are! People are getting itchy! Wanna hear from their preacher!

SAM: The preacher is busy trying to open this door!

GRACIE: Thought you was praying?

SAM: And praying to our Lord and savior—I'm multitasking.

GRACIE: Them keys ain't working?

SAM: No, Gracie. They ain't working.

GRACIE: Huh. Maybe you should try these ones.

She has fetched a small bucket full of keys.

SAM: Those are different keys?

GRACIE: Looks like it.

SAM: Why didn't you give me those keys when you gave me these?!

GRACIE: Shoot! I'm so distracted lately. My poor husband George—

SAM: Bless him.

GRACIE: Well, it's official, he has the worst case of shingles the doctors have ever seen! They're writing a paper about him!

(SAM's basically just one big shingle at this point.)

(GRACIE indicates her body, butt, crotch, etc.)

SAM: I can't heal hi—

GRACIE: I know. He don't take to healing for some reason—

SAM: Sorry—

GRACIE: You healed just about everybody else in the congregation though!

SAM: I was on a roll.

GRACIE: Put your hands on my head, said "Be Healed!" and I exploded back from the power of the Lord—

SAM: Yes—

GRACIE: Crashed into a wall!

SAM: Yeah—

GRACIE: Nearly broke my hip but my Glaucoma was healed! Praise Jesus!

SAM: Uh-huh.

GRACIE: That's when I knew you was the real deal!

SAM: That's nice— Now I have to…

GRACIE: Oh, yeah! I'll skedaddle.

SAM: I'll pray for George—

GRACIE: Oh, don't bother. It'll all be over soon enough…The Rapture.

SAM: Right! Yes. There are no shingles in heaven, my child.

GRACIE: That's music to my ears. God is good! And to think we're all about to meet him! Who do you think he looks like? I'm thinking Wilford Brimley.

SAM: That's as good a guess as any—

GRACIE: —Without the diabetes but just as handsome.

SAM: Can we have a little privacy…

He points up.

GRACIE: OH, YES!

SAM: —to continue my holy prayers—

GRACIE: Oh! Yes! *(She steps closer to him and looks up to the Lord.)* Sorry to interrupt! *(She starts away and then stops and looks back up and points out the tray of muffins to the Lord.)* See you soon! Banana prune! *(She leaves, excited.)(*

SAM: I've got to get away from these crazy fuuu— *(He gets the door open with the first key.)* Yes! It's a miracle!

(We hear the choir again when the door opens. We also see a black bag by itself on a shelf under a strong down light.)

(Beat)

SAM: Man, this closet backs right up against the choir loft. The acoustics are incredible.

(SAM reaches for the bag and the door to the hallway opens. AL enters in a panic. The door hits SAM.)

AL: Brother, Sam!

SAM: Ah!

(The keys fly everywhere and SAM slams the closet door closed.)

AL: I know! You told me to only come in if someone was—

(MARTHA, the Church's secretary, enters. She's 48-ish, permed, and in the middle of a feverish crisis. The door hits AL.)

MARTHA: Brother Sam!

AL: Ah!

SAM: Jesus!

MARTHA: Jesus!? Where!?

SAM: No— Sorry—I was praying—

MARTHA: You are just the most devout man I have ever met.

SAM: Uh-huh—

AL: Do you want me to go forth and tend thy flock?

SAM: What?

AL: I know it is not thy flock, but that of the Christ King himself!

SAM: Uh, huh.

AL: Lo, I shall—

SAM: Al—

AL: —Tend the flock! Right. Shall, I still keep a lookout—

SAM: Tend—

AL: I know! Don't question, just—

SAM: AL—

AL: But—

SAM: Tend—

AL: Tend the flock! …Of the Lord. Christ Almighty. Okeedokee.

MARTHA: I just love the way he talks.

(AL shuts the door.)

SAM: Sister Martha—

MARTHA: I'm sorry—I had to—Brother Sam, I'm—I'm having a crisis of faith! Me! I'm a good Christian! I've always taken pride in having more faith than anyone else. You know that!

SAM: Right—

MARTHA: I was sitting in the sanctuary with everybody else just now and we're singing The Old Rugged Cross and usually I'm thinking, "Yikes, this old rugged song." Which I know is a sin since Jesus wrote it—

SAM: —Sure—

MARTHA: But it moved me for the first time. My spirit was soaring on the music which is unusual for a minor key and then I thought "I am coming to you my Lord! I'm coming! I'm coming!" You know what I mean?

SAM: Ummm—

MARTHA: But THAT made me think about this tickly thing—kind of a—a thing deep, deep in—this feeling like I've left something, something that I really need to you know, are you following me?

SAM: I don't see how I could—

MARTHA: I KNOW your testament is true. I know that any second, absolutely any moment we will be taken from this Earth! I felt the POWER when the clock struck eight. I felt the heavens shift. I felt my body become light in preparation to rise into His embrace.

SAM: Good—

MARTHA: But then as the seconds and minutes ticked by, as I waited to ascend—

SAM: There's a two hour window for this—

MARTHA: I know—

SAM: Mathematically and biblically speaking.

MARTHA: Right! I know! That's what I'm saying, I do believe with all of my soul that we are in the two hour window of when the Millennium of Christ's reign begins. I mean, duh. I'm not dumb. Your Bible math checks out as far as I'm concerned.

SAM: Can't argue with Bible math.

MARTHA: Right!?

SAM: It's like Math which is real plus, you know, the Bible—

MARTHA: Right—

SAM: —Which is also real.

MARTHA: I believe! I know that we will be raised to sit by his side sometime in the next hour and forty-five— (Checking watch) forty-three—

SAM: Forty.

MARTHA: Forty? Oh, my watch must—What do you have?

SAM: Eight Twenty.

MARTHA: Look at that. I'm slow. So… Sometime in the next hour and forty—

SAM: Thirty-nine now—

MARTHA: Ah! I know that ANY MOMENT many of us true believers will be lifted on high to be with our lord forever and ever—

SAM: Amen.

MARTHA: Amen! Praise his name!

SAM: Yeah, praise him.

MARTHA: Amen.

SAM: Amen.

MARTHA: Uh, huh. But for some reason I was still compelled to wake up this morning…and put on some very red panties for you!

SAM: Sister Martha!

MARTHA: They're real lacey.

SAM: Sister Martha!

(MARTHA *shows them.*)

MARTHA: Here they are you wanna touch 'em?

SAM: Ah! No!

MARTHA: Please! I am not done with this realm! Specifically your body! I am not done with your body!

(MARTHA*'s chasing* SAM.)

SAM: Sister Martha!

MARTHA: Please! Let's do it again!

SAM: It was a mistake the first time!

MARTHA: I wanna make the same mistake! Only this time from behind!

SAM: You're married!

MARTHA: I'm not!

SAM: Really?

MARTHA: Robbie Joe left me!

SAM: Why?

MARTHA: DoesitmatterI'maloneandIdon'twanttobealone—

SAM: I'm the Preacher and you're the church's secretary!

(MARTHA *catches* SAM.)

MARTHA: I know. Don't you want to… (*She points from his crotch to hers.*) …dictate something to me?

SAM: That's such a stretch!

MARTHA: I know! But I need you now!

SAM: You don't!

MARTHA: I do!

SAM: Martha! Mar—Martha

(SAM's *gotten a grip on* MARTHA *and slowed her down. She's doing… Something…*)

SAM: Martha—what are you doing?

MARTHA: I'm seducing you.

SAM: Why?

MARTHA: I need you.

SAM: We're in the church—

MARTHA: There's a perfect spot in the alley—

SAM: Gross—

MARTHA: —this is our last chance to do it—

(MARTHA*'s thrown him on the couch.*)

SAM: That's debatable!

MARTHA: Oh— Wait— What do you mean it's debatable? Is there— Is there a problem with the rapture?

SAM: No— No, I'm sure the Rapture will go off without a hitch.

MARTHA: The prophecy—

SAM: —It's sound. It's definite. The world is ending.

MARTHA: Oh…well… That's good.

(MARTHA *straddles* SAM *and starts to kiss him He stops her.*)

SAM: Now— It's— It's debatable that there won't be… you know…up there. In fact, I believe that there will be…you know…once we're up there.

(MARTHA *takes a second, gasps, and slaps* SAM.)

SAM: Oww!

(MARTHA *kisses* SAM.)

MARTHA: I'm sorry. It's just this flesh, Oh, God, this wicked flesh— (*She kisses him again and then slaps him again.*) How do you know that we will be able to…you know, up there?

SAM: Matthew— "On earth as it is in heaven"…

MARTHA: The Lord's prayer is about doin…?

SAM: God is telling us that everything we enjoy here will be available to us there.

MARTHA: Really?

SAM: Absolutely.

MARTHA: Even the sins.

SAM: Even the sins.

(MARTHA *gasps.*)

MARTHA: Even... (*She whispers to him.*)

SAM: Well...maybe not that—

MARTHA: Can we make babies there?

SAM: I don't know—

MARTHA: Then Heaven can wait! (*She ravishes his ear.*)

SAM: Sister Martha! Your tongue is so wet!

MARTHA: It's wet for you, baby!

(SAM *breaks away.*)

SAM: What's gotten into you?

MARTHA: I know. It's shameful but...I'm a real woman with real needs and, and I used to be a Methodist, so...I mean, I'm kinda loose. Brother Sam, this church— before you got here we were all fire and brimstone. But you took that away. You made us feel worthy of Heaven. You made the Trinity less confusing with your Holy Spirit/Casper the Friendly Ghost analogy. And then your Bible math had us getting to Heaven without dying. What's not to love? But Robbie Joe was my fifth husband. Fifth! And he was so gross. All I ever wanted was unconditional love and all I got was a bunch of nasty, smelly men. I never had a baby...I wanna go up there pregnant...I wanna Heaven baby. And the truth is, I've wanted you since your first sermon on Shadrack, Meshack, and Obendigo. Say Shadrack, Meshack, and Obendigo.

SAM: Shadrack, Meshack, and Obendigo.

MARTHA: Meow.

(MARTHA *kisses* SAM'*s ear again. He pulls away.*)

SAM: We can wait—

MARTHA: We can't! Has to be now!

SAM: Ow— Ow— We have to hold off.

MARTHA: You want me?

SAM: Sister Martha, I want your body, real bad. But now, you need to go back to the sanctuary. Sing. Pray. And then about an hour and a half from now we'll be really going at it.

MARTHA: In heaven—

SAM: In heaven.

MARTHA: Like animals.

SAM: Like filthy animals! It's gonna be like Mutual of Omaha's Wild Kingdom up there.

(Maybe SAM *and* MARTHA *make a couple of animal noises at each other.)*

MARTHA: GRRR… Nope, too sexy. Gotta do it now!

SAM: I can't because… Wait! Yes, Lord? The Lord is speaking to me.

*(*MARTHA *gasps.)*

SAM: Uh, huh. Uh huh. Sure. I won't. That's great news Lord, thanks! You, too.

MARTHA: What?

SAM: You're gonna like this. Someone else in this church is your soulmate and I promised I wouldn't say who.

MARTHA: I gotta soulmate here?

SAM: Yes. *(He places his arm around Martha's shoulder and fans out his other hand in front of them, envisioning, painting a mental picture.)* I can see it so clearly, my child. Like it's happening right in front of my eyes.

MARTHA: Am I on top?

SAM: No, child. Your afterlife.

MARTHA: You mean…in heaven?

SAM: It starts here. He is going to surprise you before the Rapture and sweep you off your feet with a big show of affection and true love—

MARTHA: True love! You're not jealous after what we had?

SAM: Nope.

MARTHA: We're going to meet and...

SAM: He'll give you a baby—

MARTHA: Really?!

SAM: Yep.

MARTHA: Wow!

SAM: So, you just make yourself available to him by... getting away from me, okay?

MARTHA: Okay... (*She starts to leave and stops at the door to that leads to the sanctuary.*) I just want so much from this world before, you know—

SAM: I understand, my child.

MARTHA: Is that bad?

SAM: Not at all.

MARTHA: okay. Well...we'll always have that time together—

SAM: Okay—

MARTHA: At the Dairy Queen—

SAM: —All right—

MARTHA: In the bathroom.

SAM: Yes.

(*When* MARTHA *shuts the door* SAM *tries the closet door and it's locked again.*)

SAM: No!

(SAM *grabs the key bucket and starts trying keys.* GRACIE *enters with a stack of magazines and another bowl of keys.*)

GRACIE: Here let me…

(GRACIE *pours the bowl of keys out into the bucket of keys. She starts to exit, setting the magazines down on her way out but never stops.* SAM *follows her. Maybe he's contemplating strangling her?*)

SAM: Ah! Ah!

GRACIE: No need to thank me!

SAM: Gracie!

GRACIE: Just like to help!

SAM: Stop! Helping!

GRACIE: Can't! It's how I'm wired! I been doing nothing but help since George's ingrown hair on his back turned septic on our honeymoon! Forty years later and it's still weeping like you know who—

(SAM *slams the door in* GRACIE's *face. Simultaneously, the door to the hall opens and* ROBIN *enters.*)

ROBIN: Sam!

SAM: Ah!

ROBIN: I got the crackers—

SAM: Fine, Robin, fine—

Brother Sam goes to Robin to hurry him out.

ROBIN: —and the wine—

SAM: Uh huh—

ROBIN: For the communion—

SAM: That's great—

ROBIN: I know I'm just the Youth Minister—

SAM: You have my blessing—

ROBIN: I got real wine this time if that's okay—

SAM: Okay.

ROBIN: Feel like that counts mor'n juice—

SAM: Yep. Go do it—

Sam has led Robin to a door.

ROBIN: Is it in bad taste that the wine is Menage Trois?

SAM: Nah.

ROBIN: You think?

SAM: Father, Son, and the Holy Ghost.

ROBIN: Ohhh!! You sure that's not in bad ta—

(SAM *slams the door on* ROBIN. AL *rushes in. The door slams into* SAM.)

SAM: AH!

AL: What did Martha want?

SAM: She wanted to have sex with me!

AL: That's bad!

SAM: Yeah! No man is safe around her. I wouldn't even want to be the arm of a couch around her.

AL: A romantic entanglement would divert our mission.

SAM: Yeah.

AL: And the mission is all.

SAM: The mission is everything.

AL: Right.

SAM: These people have gone insane!

AL: Everybody is all jumpy. This Rapture can't come soon enough.

(*Beat*)

SAM: Al—you— You're clear that there is no Rapture, right?

AL: Oh. Right—

SAM: It's just a cover for my sudden departure.

AL: Our—

SAM: Our sudden departure—

AL: Right. I don't understand why but I don't have to understand, I have to have—

SAM: —Faith. Right—

AL: And when we leave this time we're going—

SAM: —at the same time. Absolutely.

AL: Good. We're partners—

SAM: —Well, you're my sidekick. And BEST buddy!

AL: Good.

SAM: Help me with these keys. You hand 'em and I'll try 'em.

(They get in a rhythm of AL handing SAM a key, SAM tries it, hands it back to AL who drops the key right back into the pile and hands him another. Sometimes AL doesn't even drop them. They just end up handing the same two keys back and forth.)

AL: Hey, Sam, can I talk to you about something that's been weighing mightily on my heart?

SAM: Weighing mightily on your— You're talking like one of these people.

AL: Habit, I guess. I kinda like them. Don't you?

SAM: …Sure. They have their charms.

AL: I know you said to not get too involved—

SAM: —Right—

AL: —in people's lives who are off mission… And I am on mission! You know, I am—

SAM: I know.

AL: Every mission! Every stop we make I am right behind you.

SAM: Yep.

AL: You're my best friend in the whole wide world and I'd do anything for you—

SAM: I know—

AL: Like when you were an injured trapeze artist and I was a bearded lady?

SAM: Uh-huh.

AL: I never wavered. Performed every show. And on the Grand Canyon Railway? I was the one who thought to switch that dynamite for carrots in the first place.

SAM: Saved our bacon.

AL: I'm always right there for you.

SAM: I know you are, Al. It's something I love about you. Your loyalty.

AL: I am loyal like a dog. You bet I am. And on mission at ALL times but there's something here that is bothering me.

SAM: I'm listening.

AL: There's a woman—

(SAM *stops.*)

SAM: Al!

AL: Not like that! It's Ruth.

SAM: The part-time accountant?

AL: She's real nice—

SAM: She's beloved around here—why is that?

AL: She's really genuine and honest and sweet and so pretty—

SAM: Al, we can't have romantic entanglements—

AL: I know—I haven't had a romantic entanglement in all the years we've been doing this—

SAM: I know.

AL: And you know how fond I am of romantic entanglements—

SAM: You love 'em.

AL: Right… But we have gotten to know each other a little—

SAM: AL!

AL: And listen to this! I believe that her husband is not nice!

SAM: He's not nice?

AL: Not one bit!

SAM: What does that have to do with us?

AL: He just—I just hate to see a nice person in a real bad situation with a not nice person!

SAM: I know you do. Gosh, I love you, little guy. I love your compassion. I love how ticklish you are—

(A very quick tickle)

AL: Stop! Ah!

SAM: I love it. But the church's part-time accountant's marital troubles are not part of our concern here. *(He goes back to trying keys.)* Right now, the only thing we need to focus on is getting in this closet—

AL: But—

SAM: Al, I'm going to level with you. There's a eighty-eight percent chance our mission fails if we don't get in here in the next half hour.

AL: Eighty-eight percent!?

SAM: Eighty-eight.

AL: Then we have to get in there! What's in there?

SAM: A bag.

AL: What's in the bag?

SAM: Have faith, Al.

AL: Yeah.

SAM: All will be revealed.

AL: I know. I love you, Sam.

SAM: I love you, too, buddy—

(SAM's *handed* AL *another key that he drops right into the bucket before fetching another.*)

SAM: Are— Are you just dropping the keys I've tried back into the same pile you got them from?

(Beat)

AL: Shoot.

SAM: Al—

AL: Shoot!

SAM: —I had it open a minute ago—

AL: Al, ya dummy! I'm real sorry—

(The door to the hall opens and GRACIE *comes back in.)*

GRACIE: Brother Sam! Come quick! Snuffy McWilliams has been raptured!

SAM: What!?

AL: Really?!

GRACIE: Yes!

AL: *(To* SAM*)* It's real!?

SAM: No, Al! Of course not!

GRACIE: It's not!?

SAM: Yes, Gracie! Of course, it is!

AL: It is!?

SAM: Oh, for the love of God. Gracie, what happened?

GRACIE: The whole congregation is going crazy! "Why take him lord!? Why not me?! Snuffy McWilliams is divorced!"

AL: He disappeared?

GRACIE: It's crazy. The last thing anyone heard him say was "I gotta pee". A minute later he had vanished without a trace.

(Beat)

SAM: ...Have you checked the bathroom?

GRACIE: No. What in the world is your point?! The congregation is goin' nuttier than a porta-potty at a peanut festival!

SAM: Ah—dang—

GRACIE: There's a revolt! Evan Hatfield is threatening a walkout! He used to be a Unitarian! He believes in nothing!

SAM: I—all right! All right!

(SAM and AL follow GRACIE into the hall. As soon as they're gone, TROY, an earnest young man of 20 and TONYA, a 21 year-old woman, peer in from the kitchen.)

TONYA: They gone?

TROY: Yeah.

TONYA: What did you need to talk about, Troy? You're scaring me. Where did you run off to half-cocked—

TROY: Tonya— You know how I feel about that phrase—

TONYA: Too stimulating.

TROY: Right.

TONYA: Sorry.

(TROY *takes* TONYA *by the hands.*)

TROY: Tonya, you know how much I love you.

TONYA: Yes. And I—I love you, Troy.

TROY: We've been together for almost a year now, Tonya. What we have, well, it's like, special or something. Right?

TONYA: Um, sure, Troy. Yeah.

TROY: And I've always been a gentleman.

TONYA: Of course.

TROY: You said you wanted to wait until marriage.

TONYA: Right.

TROY: And I have kept myself totally pure, my entire life.

TONYA: Right— Right—me too.

TROY: TOTALLY pure, Tonya. I ain't done nothing. I said my purity pledge when I was eight.

TONYA: Right.

TROY: Tonya…I've never even done that bad thing that—that guys do…alone.

TONYA: Really? Troy, you're twenty-five! You're gonna explode!

TROY: I KNOW!! I'm super pure, Tonya!

TONYA: Right…um, me too!

TROY: You're the picture of purity! So perfect and virginal—

TONYA: Uh huh…

TROY: Well, with this rapture coming down on us like this, it's got me thinking. Tonya, I—I don't want to

be called home to live with Jesus without ever…you
know…

TONYA: I feel the same. I don't want to go without
experiencing…you know…one last time. Or…one time,
I mean…ever…the only time…one time. Just once. I
haven't one it before. You'd be the first.

TROY: Right. So, I was thinking… *(He gets down on one
knee.)*

TONYA: Troy, what are you doing?

TROY: Isn't it obvious?

TONYA: No. You got down on one knee to ask me out
on a date. And to give me a purity ring. And to ask me
to your family's Thanksgiving dinner. There were a lot
of times, actually.

(TROY pulls out a piece of paper and shakes it loose.)

TROY: This time it's for real, Tonya. That's where I
disappeared to. My cousin's a county clerk. I got us
a license. I want to marry you, Tonya. That way, we
can, um…consummate things. I really, really want to
consummate, Tonya.

TONYA: Yeah?

TROY: I want to consummate so bad.

TONYA: Troy—

TROY: I feel if I don't do some consummating real soon
I'm gonna become a serial killer!

TONYA: Troy, we can just consummate! Right now.
Without any-—

TROY: Tonya, no! If we have consummations without
this paper signed by the proper authorities, then we'll
go the hell! We have to do it right to keep our purity
that I know both of us hold so dear.

TONYA: Riiigghhht…

(TROY *pulls out a very small ring from his pocket.*)

TONYA: You have a ring?! Where did you get a ring?!

TROY: From Jared.

TONYA: You went to Jared's?!

TROY: Yeah! I told you! My cousin, Jared! The county clerk? He has a drawer full of rings. It's a package deal.

TONYA: But we only have an hour and fifteen minutes.

(TROY *looks at his watch.*)

TROY: I have an hour and ten.

(TONYA *and* TROY *both look at their watches.*)

TONYA: Ah!

(*But how would we…*)

TROY: Tonya, all I have to do is track down Brother Sam, and he can marry us right on the spot. Then we can…

TONYA: Consummate?

TROY: All over the place.

(TROY *puts away the license and leaves the ring with* TONYA. *He starts out. He awkwardly stops short.*)

TONYA: Are you, okay?

TROY: Yeah. I just shouldn't have worn corduroy today. Too stimulating… You know, I've dreamed about this day all my life.

TONYA: I know you have, Troy.

TROY: All the clippings from the—

TONYA: —wedding magazines. Yeah. I remember. You mailed them to me.

TROY: There is nothing more beautiful than two people who have saved themselves for each other—

TONYA: Troy, I'm sorry. I—I …

TROY: Sorry for what, Tonya?

TONYA: I know I'm not…I mean…the ceremony. This is not what you've always dreamed of. It's not like your—your—

TROY: Wedding collage.

TONYA: Right.

TROY: Oh, Tonya. It's not about that. It's about—

TONYA: Love.

TROY: Getting married real quick.

TONYA: And…love…and me? Right?

TROY: What? Of course. Yes. You. And me. And love. Of course, sweetheart. Real quick. Now, you go get ready to get married. Do your hair all pretty—

TONYA: —I spent an hour—

TROY: —and put on some makeup—

TONYA: —I have on makeup—

TROY: —and find something pretty to wear.

TONYA: —This is my favorite dress.

TROY: Because while you do that, I'm going to find Brother Sam. And then he's going to make this all official. *(He stops in the door.)* We'll be married, Tonya. Married under the eyes of God. Joined in holy matrimony in the name of Jesus Christ our Lord and Savior and then we can go out back in the alley by the dumpster and hump like two homeless dogs…in love.

(TROY hurries away. TONYA stares at the ring on her finger with a mixture of emotions: she is touched, but very worried about something. After a beat, she exits in the opposite direction as TROY.)

(RUTH enters, glancing around nervously. She has the remnants of a week old black eye. She is holding an empty

*black bag that has "3rd Baptist Church of Uncertain, TX"
printed on the side. She crosses to the closet and reaches for
the door, but pauses and turns away. She looks conflicted,
but then hoists the bag under her arm to check its weight. It
is too light. She scurries to the magazine rack/bookshelf and
lays the bag out open on the surface. She begins gathering up
the magazines Gracie had left and placing them in the bag
until she lifts it again checking its weight. She is surprised
by* MARTHA *entering the room.* RUTH *throws the bag under
a table.)*

MARTHA: Well, hey there Ruth. I'm surprised you're
still around. Figured you'd be the first one Raptured to
be with the Lord.

RUTH: *(Momentary panic, looking at watch.)* What? No.
No, I've got an hour and five minutes left.

*(*MARTHA *taps her watch.)*

MARTHA: I swear to both Sugarbaker sisters, this thing
keeps jumping around like a two-tailed cat. What
happened to your eye?

RUTH: Hm? Doorknob.

MARTHA: Ah.

RUTH: I don't—I don't know why you think that I
would be taken first.

MARTHA: Ha! Oh, sweetie. You're sweeter than pie.
You haven't seen Brother Sam around have you?

RUTH: No. No, not lately.

MARTHA: Or any other men?

RUTH: No men.

MARTHA: Dang. Okay, well, listen…I have it on good
authority that we have a little more time. Something
has been foretold.

RUTH: Okay.

MARTHA: Something involving me.

RUTH: Great.

MARTHA: And a man.

RUTH: Okay.

MARTHA: I'm on my way to get a little somethin' somethin' from my desk…

RUTH: Okay.

MARTHA: Something secret…

RUTH: Great.

MARTHA: Ha. Wouldn't you like to know.

(MARTHA's gone. RUTH *pulls the bag back out, obviously a touch conflicted now. She checks the weight and grabs a few more magazines. As she is putting them in the bag,* GRACIE *enters holding a mop and a slippery floor sign.* RUTH *spins, still holding the bag and magazines.)*

RUTH: Gracie!

GRACIE: Ruth! What's the matter, sweetie? You look all nervous. Like you're right in the middle of a crisis of conscience of some sort. It's as if you're filling that bag with them magazines and are swapping it out for a bag of money! And now you're contemplating whether or not to split town with that money!

(Beat)

(GRACIE *laughs loudly and* RUTH *joins nervously.)*

GRACIE: Oh, I am a delight.

RUTH: Yes. Such a delight.

GRACIE: I've had to laugh through the tough times. My George has the rickets.

RUTH: Oh, no

GRACIE: Yep. In the right light, the bottom half of George's body looks just like Alfred Hitchcock's silhouette.

RUTH: Oh, I'm sorry.

GRACIE: It's okay. It'll all be over soon enough… Rapture!

RUTH: Right. Of course.

GRACIE: I see you're also a fan of The *O!* magazines!

(RUTH *realizes she means the magazines. They're all* O! *magazines.*)

RUTH: Oh, yeah. Love Oprah. Sorry.

GRACIE: It's okay, darlin'. I read them *O!* magazines as soon as I get 'em. Then I bring them up here to share the good word of Oprah. George reads 'em on the pot.

RUTH: Okay. Is it all right if I take these?

GRACIE: Pretty sure that's not going to matter one way or another in forty-four minutes.

(RUTH *checks her watch.*)

GRACIE: Welp. I'd better get this in there. *(She holds up the floor sign and mop.)* Sam just forbade everybody from going to the bathroom and there's a mess of enlarged prostates in there… *(She starts out.)* Hey, wait…what happened to your eye?

RUTH: What? Um…doorknob.

(Beat)

GRACIE: Okay! Well, see you later!

(GRACIE *exits.* TROY *comes in and* RUTH *shoves the bag back into hiding.*)

TROY: Ms Ruth! Have you seen Brother Sam?!

RUTH: No. I haven't seen him lately.

TROY: Darn. I need to find him real bad. What's up with the—uh—

RUTH: Oh, doorknob.

TROY: Ouch. Ms Ruth, you're—you're a good person.

RUTH: I—I'm no better than anyone else, Troy.

TROY: No way, Ms Ruth. You're a REALLY good person. Like, so good. You'll be the first to go, for sure. I mean, in fifty three minutes there will be nothing left of you but a pile of clothes. Your dress, crumpled on the floor. Bra and panties lying on— Ugh! No! I'm—I'm so sorry, Ms Ruth! I'm so wicked. I gotta find Brother Sam.

RUTH: What's wrong, Troy?

TROY: Ms Ruth, as a good Christian woman, can you give me a little advice?

RUTH: Of course.

TROY: If you were in a relationship with a person, but weren't necessarily ready to get married, but you want to go to heaven but you also really, really, really, really, really wanted to…be with that person or any person. You know…physically. Like, physically…under the clothes. Do you follow me—

RUTH: I—I do—

TROY: —I'm talking about be with this person in a Biblical sense—

RUTH: Right—

TROY: —And we are talking about the Old Testament Biblical sense. None of that soft core New Testament being with someone. I mean dirty cave being with someone. Like the just after the flood no holds barred kind of—

RUTH: Okay! I understand what you mean, Troy.

(TROY *is aroused.*)

TROY: Ah! I'm not ready to get married but I have to get married or I'm going to die! *(He hurries off as best as he can…)*

RUTH: Troy, marriage is nothing to rush—rush into!

(TROY *stops short.*)

TROY: Ah! Corduroy! Gotta find Brother Sam!

RUTH: Maybe Al could help—

(TROY's *gone.*)

(RUTH *pulls the bag back out and turns to go back to the closet. She pulls out a key and unlocks the closet, opening it wide to show an identical black bag on an upper shelf. She switches the bags, closes the closet back, and crosses to the desk/table. She opens the bag, pulling up a stack of money. She puts the money back in the bag and closes it. She steels her nerve and starts to walk out with the bag.* AL *enters.*)

AL: …Ruth…

(RUTH *freezes. She is positioned so that her body blocks* AL's *sight of the bag. She very slyly slides it down to hide it back under the desk/table before turning around. She only turns far enough towards him where he can't see her eye.*)

RUTH: Al. Hey…I…I—um, no…well, I told Troy he should…he should go find you. I think the poor boy is having a bit of a personal crisis.

AL: Yeah, he blew by me looking for Brother Sam. He was walking like—like… *(He mimics* TROY's *walk.)*

RUTH: Bless his heart. I really think you should—you should really go catch him. I think you could help him.

AL: Yeah, yeah. I will. I just wanted to talk to you first for a minute. If that's okay, I mean.

RUTH: Me? Yeah. What— What about?

AL: Ruth, I just want you to know…I want you to know that…I want you to feel like…

RUTH: Oh! Oh…Al…I do…I mean…I always…you are always…

AL: I am—I know—I mean, I'm—

RUTH: —You are. You really are.

AL: Yep.

RUTH: You're such a—

AL: I am.

RUTH: The best—

AL: I've always been very good at…

RUTH: Really. The best.

AL: And if you wanted to…

RUTH: I know. And I may…want…to…

AL: And if you do…

RUTH: If I do…

AL: Then I'll be…

RUTH: You'll be…

AL: Absolutely.

RUTH: I know. I know you will.

AL: Yep.

RUTH: Yes.

AL: Okay. Well…good talk.

RUTH: Great talk.

AL: You usually face me more directly when we talk but still…

RUTH: Great talk.

AL: *(Motioning the way* TROY *went)* Yeah…I guess I'll…

RUTH: *(She motions off in the other direction)* Yep. And I'll
…

AL: See you…

RUTH: Around.

AL: Yep.

RUTH: Al?

AL: Yeah, Ruth?

RUTH: Thanks…for being my friend.

AL: Thank you for being my friend, too.

(Pause)

(AL exits towards the sanctuary. RUTH takes the bag back out from hiding. She starts to go, but turns to look back toward AL. She looks back and forth between the bag and AL until she sighs and puts it back into hiding.)

RUTH: Oh, Al. *(She leaves to go after AL.)*

(MARTHA enters immediately carrying an identical bag to the other two. She hugs it closely.)

(She looks for a hiding place for it and settles putting under a desk. She exits towards the sanctuary.)

(As soon as the door closes, TONYA enters from the hallway door. She's distraught and sits on the floor with her back to the desk. She's crying.)

(ROBIN, the youth pastor, enters from the kitchen wiping at his pants which are soaked in the front. TONYA is hidden from him as he works on his pants for a moment.)

ROBIN: I am never going to get this out—

TONYA: Brother Robin!

ROBIN: Ah! Tonya! Where did you come from?

TONYA: I was sitting on the floor here.

ROBIN: Oh, my Lord, you gave me a heart attack.

TONYA: Sorry.

ROBIN: I thought it was some kind of reverse Rapture. People appearing outta nowhere. Lord! Are you—are you okay?

TONYA: I just needed some time alone.

ROBIN: Hey, I get it. This is a stressful time for all of us. I mean I could be called to our Lord's side at any moment and all I can think is "Not yet, Lord! Wait until my pants dry! I swear it's not pee-pee, Lord!"

TONYA: What happened?

ROBIN: Well, I was in the sanctuary serving communion for anyone who didn't think it was too Catholicy when T J Wommack stepped up, that little you know what. I'm giving him the saltine and I say "This is the Lord's body, take it in your mouth" And as a youth pastor I'm used to giggles on lines like that… but right before I could place that little cracker on his tongue he covered the Lord's body with half a can of EZ Cheese!

TONYA: Oh, no. But what about your pants?

ROBIN: Oh, my Dockers caught a spray of EZ Cheese when I slapped the hell out of him.

TONYA: Wow.

ROBIN: Everything okay with you?

TONYA: Oh, you know. Boy problems. You wouldn't understand.

ROBIN: Try me.

TONYA: I—Troy and I have been a couple, right, for a good while. And he's great. He's just the sweetest, most genuine guy.

ROBIN: What's the problem?

TONYA: Oh, it's just so…it's sexy stuff…

ROBIN: Dish, girl? I'm a Youth Pastor. I've heard everything and will keep it top secret. A young man who shall remain nameless—it was T J Wommack— He confessed to having relations with a watermelon he'd warmed up in the microwave and does that mean he's going to hell and I said "Yes, it does".

TONYA: ...Okay... Well, that helps... See, I sort of insisted on waiting to...you know...

ROBIN: Oh!?

TONYA: Yeah. He was such a gentleman but now we're regretting that and I'd be happy to have relations whenever. Unmarried.

ROBIN: But he's not.

TONYA: Right. He's got it in his head that Brother Sam could marry us real quick first but we can't find Brother Sam.

ROBIN: You don't need Brother Sam. I can do it.

TONYA: You can?

ROBIN: Yes, girl. I am a Youth Minister, Music Minister, and Minister Minister.

TONYA: That's great. You'd do that?

ROBIN: Tonya, I figure if we've only got an hour left on Earth we should make the most of it.

TONYA: Yeah?

ROBIN: Is there something else?

TONYA: Well, that's great, and I...he doesn't know everything about me—

ROBIN: Drama!

TONYA: Troy is a virgin...

ROBIN: Obvs.

TONYA: And he thinks I am.

ROBIN: Shut the front door! You're not?

TONYA: Not even close.

ROBIN: Oh, my... Anyone I know?

TONYA: Well, do you know the community college baseball team?

ROBIN: Oh, Tonya.

TONYA: Yeah. And do you know Mark Stoner?

(ROBIN *gasps.*)

ROBIN: Mark Stoner was the best looking boy in school!

TONYA: I know! And he has an insatiable appetite.

ROBIN: Oh, I just bet he does!

TONYA: I wanted to be good—to do it different with Troy. Try it the way God wants it. So, I insisted on waiting and he doesn't know I'm a filthy slut—

ROBIN: Now, girl, don't you do that to yourself! No! Do not slut shame yourself! There's plenty of so and sos out there that will do that for you. Do you love yourself even though you've let Mark Stoner and an entire community college baseball team into your private pants area?

TONYA: Well, yeah...

ROBIN: Then don't judge yourself too hard about your past.

TONYA: I've tried to pray my sexuality away but it didn't work.

ROBIN: Tell me about it!

TONYA: I'm know I'm not gonna be raptured cause of my sins—

(ROBIN *hugs* TONYA.)

ROBIN: Oh, Tonya—

TONYA: Will Troy love me if I'm honest about who I am!?

ROBIN: Tonya, I understand your situation—being in love with one man but afraid to tell him about the countless other men you've been with.

TONYA: Oh, yeah?

ROBIN: Yes, girl. Well, I can picture myself in that situation—except with some sexy ladies— So, I get it. And darn it all I'm gonna help you with this!

TONYA: Really!?

ROBIN: I think everyone should be able to love who and how they want as long as it isn't hurting anyone else and the only person I know in this town who agrees with me is my roommate, Clark!

TONYA: It's okay—

ROBIN: I might as well be an Episcopalian without all the damned idolatry—

TONYA: Oh, Robin—

ROBIN: I have confession. There's something about me…that's gonna keep me from being raptured!

TONYA: What?!

ROBIN: Tonya—I'm…I identify as…Tonya, I'm a liberal!!

TONYA: Oh, no!

ROBIN: I was born this way!

TONYA: Liberalism is a choice!

ROBIN: Well, I can't help how I think! I want people to enjoy life!

TONYA: I want to enjoy life!

ROBIN: Me too! And I know God hates that but sometimes… Darn it all, I don't care what he thinks!

(ROBIN *and* TONYA *gasp! Then they comfort each other.*)

ROBIN: Tonya, you are beautiful, and strong, and sexy. And all of that is okay as far as I'm concerned.

TONYA: Thank you! You are sweet and kind and that's okay with me.

ROBIN: Tonya. Let's do this. Let's get you married so you can rock that boy's world!

TONYA: Yeah!

ROBIN: I want you to live your best life for the next sixty-three minutes.

TONYA: Yeah!

ROBIN: You go find Troy and tell him to meet us here in twenty minutes. I'll get things set up in here for post wedding shenanigans. Then you go get yourself ready to come out to him as the fierce queen you are!

TONYA: How?

ROBIN: Slap on some makeup—

TONYA: I'm wear—

ROBIN: Dress up in something nice—

TONYA: This is my—

ROBIN: Pop in your Nuvaring—

TONYA: It's in.

ROBIN: I see you busting in here with a big passionate speech with no apologies. I'm here! I love men's bodies! The chests! The butts! The whole thing! Get used to it!

TONYA: Yeah!

ROBIN: Good?

TONYA: Good! Thank you, Brother Robin!

ROBIN: Now, let's shag ass! Sorry— Booty!

(ROBIN *and* TONYA *exit. A window opens and* DICK,
RUTH's *husband, climbs through it. He's a rough looking*
guy. He has a beard, wears his long hair back in a pony tail,
and carries a large knife on his hip. He searches the room
for a moment. He opens the closet door and begins to look
around, but a door opens behind him and he closes himself
inside. TROY *enters frantically.)*

TROY: Sam?! Brother Sam?!? *(He checks his watch.)*
Aargh! I'm running out of time! Lord? Lord I need
your help. I need to find Brother Sam, Lord. I need to
get married.

(DICK *speaks loudly from the closet. The voice of God)*

DICK: Marriage is overrated, kid.

*(*TROY *gasps!)*

TROY: Lord?!? Is that you?!?

DICK: Umm…sure.

TROY: You— You've never talked back before.

DICK: Well, you got me on the line. Shoot.

TROY: Uh— Okay— Uh— Lord, all I've ever dreamed
about since I was a boy was getting married. And I've
kept myself totally pure—

DICK: What do you mean totally pure?

TROY: Lord, you know what I mean. I never…

DICK: Never?

TROY: Not once.

DICK: Nothing? Not even with yourself?

TROY: I pee sitting down so I won't…touch it and
tempt myself.

DICK: Kid, you're gonna explode.

TROY: I know, Lord! I KNOW!

DICK: Kid, remember, where two or more are gathered in my name there are three more skipping church to whack it.

TROY: I've never heard it like that…

DICK: Well, now you have.

TROY: God, I need you to help me find Sam! I need to get married!

DICK: You don't need that. Just do it. Have a ball.

TROY: Do…it? It, Lord? Without marriage?

DICK: Sure. I saw an alley out back that——

TROY: But, Lord. That's not what…all my life I've thought…how will I…how will I know when to…

DICK: Whip it out?

TROY: If it pleases you lord, yes. My father who art in heaven, how shall I know when to whip it out?

DICK: All I know is don't send a picture of it. No one wants that. It's not photogenic. Just wait for a very clear sign.

TROY: A sign?!? You'll send me a sign, Lord?!?

DICK: Huh? Me? Um… Ha, yeah, I'll send a sign.

TROY: Thank you! Thank you, Lord. I shall wait for your sign. Thank you! Thank you!

(TROY *hurries out the door opposite the sanctuary door, still thanking the Lord and muttering Amen.* DICK *opens the door but the door to the sanctuary opens and he closes himself in again.* SAM *enters carrying a plate of muffins. He is yelling back to the congregation.)*

SAM: I'm just saying that God doesn't want anyone else to go to the bathroom without announcing it first! And announcing the number, number one or two, will let people know how long to expect you to be gone! And no more muffins!

(SAM *shuts the door and hurries to the closet. He grabs the knob and opens it to find* DICK.)

DICK: Hey.

SAM: Jesus!

DICK: No. Dick.

SAM: Well, there's no need for insults.

DICK: No. I'm Dick.

SAM: Ah. I'm very sorry.

DICK: Who are you?

SAM: Me?

DICK: You.

SAM: Sam.

DICK: Brother Sam…I know all about you, Preacher Man.

SAM: Oh? Muffin, my Child? They're banana prune. Gracie thought everyone should get cleaned out before going to heaven.

DICK: Right…your rapture.

SAM: Aha. 'Tis not my rapture but that of the lord, our god.

DICK: Uh-huh. Have you seen Ruth?

SAM: Ruth— Oh, Dick—

DICK: I'm Ruth's Dick.

SAM: Oh, ha, that sounds like you're her—

DICK: I'm looking for her. Have you seen her?

SAM: I—uh, I—Ruth—

DICK: Do you know what part of the church Ruth is in?

SAM: No. I—Al, saw her in here earlier.

DICK: In here? Al? Brother Al?

SAM: Yeah, Al.

DICK: Wait, you saw her in here? Or Al saw her in here? Or you saw them together in here?

SAM: Yes.

DICK: Which one?

SAM: I'm sorry?

DICK: One or both?

SAM: I don't follow.

DICK: Look, Buddy. Will you just go find Ruth and tell her something for me? Tell her, I know.

SAM: I know?

DICK: Yeah.

SAM: What is it that I know—

DICK: —I. I know.

SAM: Oh— YOU know.

DICK: Brother Sam, are you a stupid person?

SAM: Huh?

DICK: Right. Tell her I know she's trying to dick me over and Dick doesn't like to be dicked.

SAM: Umm… Well, my child, I'm kind of busy with the Lord's wahhh—

(DICK twists SAM's hand.)

DICK: Listen, dude. I will kick every tooth out of your head. You hear me?

SAM: Yes.

DICK: It will take several kicks.

SAM: I would not like that to happen.

DICK: Then go tell her.

SAM: Yeah.

DICK: Now.

SAM: Yes, sir.

(SAM *exits.* DICK *inspects the closet and opens it. He grabs the bag and tests its weight.*)

DICK: Holy hell. She wasn't kidding.

(ROBIN *backs into the room from the kitchen. He's overloaded with several things; a down comforter, a set of sheets, candles, a small bag, a pillow, etc.* DICK *closes himself into the closet.*)

ROBIN: Okey dokey.

(ROBIN *looks around the room and drops his burden off. He grabs the desk that* MARTHA *hid her bag under and moves it more central in the room. The bag is exposed but he doesn't notice it. He sings to the tune of* Like A Virgin *while he works. He covers the table with the comforter as a cushion. Then he does two layers of sheets. He reaches in the small bag, which is full of rose petals, and liberally sprinkles them all over the scene.*)

ROBIN:
They're so young and they're fine
Do what they want 'til the end of time
Which is in an hour
Which is in an hour...please rapture me lord
Like a virgin (hey!)
He'll be touched for the very first time...
(He turns and sees the bag.) That wasn't there a second...
Lord? Did you? *(He's opened the bag and snaps it shut again. He looks to the heavens. He pulls out a red feather boa.)* A red feather boa... *(He pulls out a dildo...)*

ROBIN: A...AH! *(He throws it back in the bag...then he takes out a huge bottle of lube.)* What do we have here? A big ol' bottle of lube! *(He looks to the heavens.)* Lord!? Does this mean my work here is righteous? You truly work in mysterious and I guess sometimes kind of gross ways. Have at it kiddos.

(ROBIN *set the bag on the table. The door opens and he ducks behind the table.* AL *and* RUTH *enter.*)

AL: That's a pretty tall doorknob is all I'm say—

RUTH: Al.

AL: You'd have to open it—like this.

RUTH: —Al, please. Just forget about my eye.

AL: But you're hurt—

RUTH: I'm fine. Forget it. Forget. It.

AL: What's wrong?

RUTH: Hey, sorry—

AL: Is everything okay?

RUTH: It's—I'm— It's not. It's not okay.

AL: You got me worried.

RUTH: Sorry— It's going to be okay. It will.

AL: Is it about your husband?

RUTH: No—well. No. It's about this—this odd—the Rapture.

AL: Oh… What about it?

RUTH: How do you feel about it?

AL: How—? It's what everybody wants, right? It's— It's good, right?

RUTH: Is it good? When you look at the congregation in there what do you see?

AL: I see good Christia—

RUTH: Forget that. The people. What do you see in them, since Sam told us about the Rapture?

AL: I don't think I'm—

RUTH: Tell me what you see.

AL: Well, some people are WAY into it and excited and dancing around. Everybody else is…scared they won't get to go because they've been hiding who they really are.

RUTH: Which are you?

(AL's clearly talking about RUTH.)

AL: I guess…I guess I'm a little…disappointed at the timing of the whole thing. Like some people see the world as ugly and hard…and it is, I guess. I don't blame them. But I see that as a price for all the beauty. I don't want it to end.

(Pause)

RUTH: What kind of person am I?

AL: …Maybe you're looking to go to a better place. Like there's nothing left for you here anymore.

(Pause)

RUTH: How well do you know Brother Sam?

AL: Hey! Look at that! Hand sanitizer. *(He starts sanitizing his hands with lube. Trying to cleanse himself because of the lies he's telling.)* Sam? Good. Real good. Pretty good.

RUTH: I think…I know there's something going on with him.

AL: Ha! Nothing could be going on with Brother Sam— *(He puts more hand sanitizer on. All the way up his arms.)*

RUTH: That's just the thing… Haven't you thought any of this was weird? As soon as he becomes preacher he starts healing people and telling them what they want to hear and preaching that the Rapture is coming and no other church is saying that and he tells us not to tell anyone else—

AL: He had a revelation—

RUTH: Then he had us giving twenty percent instead of ten! Why do we need to donate at all if the world—

(AL *slathers on more. Puts it around his neck*)

AL: Sorry. I just feel so dirty.

RUTH: Nothing has been repaired. Bills haven't been paid…

AL: I don't know what—

RUTH: Where has that money gone? Where are the donations from the last several months? They're not in the bank.

AL: What're you trying to say, Ruth?

RUTH: I know you and Brother Sam have gotten close.

AL: We have.

RUTH: But how well do you know him?

AL: Look, he's a saint, okay? In all the years I've known him he's been nothing but upstanding.

RUTH: Really?

AL: Yeah.

RUTH: I thought you met him this year here at the church.

AL: Hm?

RUTH: You moved here from Louisiana and he moved here from Abilene close to the same time.

AL: Year. In all the year I've known him. I misspoke. Because I'm dumb. Which is more proof that I'm from Louisiana.

RUTH: …So, you trust Brother Sam?

AL: I do.

(*Beat*)

RUTH: Al, I like you.

AL: I like you, too.

RUTH: You're kind.

AL: You, too.

RUTH: And sweet.

AL: You, too.

RUTH: You're a good man.

AL: You, too.

RUTH: And I don't want to see you get hurt.

AL: I don't like to get hurt.

RUTH: So, there's nothing, in your opinion, off about Brother Sam?

(Pause)

AL: Uh, nope. Gotta—gotta have faith in Brother Sam.

(Beat)

RUTH: Well…okay. *(She goes and fetches her bag from where she hid it.)*

AL: Where are you going?

RUTH: Just out.

AL: Will you be back before the Rapture?

RUTH: I don't think so.

AL: Oh.

RUTH: Goodbye, Al.

AL: Umm… See you later…

(RUTH leaves. After a few moments, DICK, quietly comes out of the closet. AL doesn't notice him.)

AL: Ah, Ruth…I love you. I LOVE YOU! And if I ever meet your mean old husband I'm gonna pop him.

DICK: She'll break your heart, chief.

AL: AH!

DICK: I guarantee it.

AL: Where'd you come from?

DICK: Reverse rapture. So, you're in love?

AL: What?

DICK: You're in love with Ruth there?

AL: I—um—uh…

DICK: You are the least verbal bunch of sumbitches I've ever come across.

AL: Ahh…yep.

DICK: Listen, Al, I know all about you and Sam and Ruth and this here Rapture. I know she's all hot and bothered by you—

AL: She's hot and bothered?

DICK: Yep.

AL: By me?

DICK: Hard to figure now that I see you. She thinks you're some kind of escape hatch to fly the coop with. That sound good to you?

AL: Little of a mixed metaphor, but yeah.

DICK: You and her jump in a pick up truck never to be seen or heard from again! You like the sound of that?

AL: We both drive sedans but yes!

DICK: I thought so!

AL: How do you know all of this?

DICK: She talks in her sleep.

AL: I'm sorry—

DICK: She sleeps next to me at night…because she is my wife…

AL: You're...

DICK: Dick.

AL: Ruth's Dick?

DICK: You could say that.

AL: Oh...I see...

(AL *might pop* DICK *but instead takes off and* DICK *is after him.* DICK *grabs* AL's *arm but with an audible "Squish" sound* AL *slides free. They're both confused.* DICK *grabs his other arm with the same result.* DICK *chases* AL *and catches him, putting both hands around his neck.* AL *screams and turns 360 and we hear the "Squish" sound.* DICK *can't choke him! He's too lubed!*)

(*Finally* DICK *gets a hold on* AL.)

DICK: I'm about to ditch town, too. Every other time in my life I've ditched town it's because I've beaten someone half to death. Not sure why this time should be any different.

(ROBIN *jumps out of hiding and onto* DICK's *back.*)

ROBIN: Bonzai!

DICK: Ah! What the—I been Pearl Harbored!

(AL *joins in the fight. He and* ROBIN *together are giving* DICK *a good tousle but* DICK *stays pretty well in control. They end up behind the table* ROBIN *had prepared. Sometimes they're visible and sometimes they go down behind the table. We see a hand strangling* ROBIN. *He disappears and* AL *pops up on the other side being strangled. He disappears and they both pop up being strangled. They disappear and* DICK *pops up being strangled by four hands. He disappears and they all appear strangling each other.* DICK *knocks* ROBIN *back and turns his attention to* AL. ROBIN *grabs a wicker basket and slams it down on* DICK's *head. It sticks there but doesn't phase him.* AL *goes down to his knees and disappears behind the table as* DICK *bends to*) *strangle him.* ROBIN *grabs* DICK *around the waist and starts pulling on him. It looks lewd to say the least.)*

ROBIN: You let him go you—you bad boy!

*(*GRACIE *enters and grabs her heart! The men don't notice her.)*

ROBIN: You bad boy! Bad, bad boy!

*(*GRACIE*'s surprise fades.)*

GRACIE: Well, I guess I'm not that surprised.

*(*AL *rises and* DICK *pushes him back down.)*

DICK: No ya don't! Get back down there!

GRACIE: Okay, NOW I'm surprised.

*(*AL *tries to break free and turns away from* DICK. DICK *grabs him around the waist.)*

DICK: I'm not done with you!

*(*DICK *pulls* AL *back violently.* SAM *enters.)*

GRACIE: *(To* SAM*)* Oh, I'm not in line.

SAM: What the…?

(All the men disappear behind the table.)

GRACIE: And THAT'S why I made George quit the Lion's Club.

*(*GRACIE *exits.* SAM *sees the bag that* ROBIN *found and is shocked to see it sitting out. He thinks it's his money. He sneaks over and grabs it. He takes off his vestment and underneath he's wearing a tear away suit which he tears off like a basketball player. He lays the clothes on the floor and then takes off his shoes and puts them next to them, pulls a pair of tighty whiteys out of his shoe and lays that on top of it all. He's still hidden on the other side of the table when* DICK *pops up.)*

DICK: That was as fun as wrasslin' with my sisters, but play time's over boys. *(He takes out his knife.)* Now, this is gonna hurt—

(SAM *pops up and knocks him out with the bag.* DICK *collapses.* AL *and* ROBIN *scream.* SAM *hustles out.* AL *pops up with blood on his hands. He screams.* ROBIN *pops up with blood on his hands. He screams. They scream.)*

AL: He's dead…

ROBIN: I don't know my own strength, I guess.

AL: You killed Ruth's husband.

ROBIN: We…killed Ruth's husband.

(AL *looks at his bloody hands.)*

AL: You're right! We killed Ruth's husband! *(Beat)* I have mixed feelings!

(Blackout)

END OF ACT ONE

ACT TWO

(Lights up on the empty fellowship hall. Beat. Dick's head pops up from behind the table. Then Al and Robin appear from behind the table. They're trying to lift him and struggling. They've wrapped him in one of the sheets from the table. They manage to get him up.)

AL: Where can we hide him?

ROBIN: Where would I hide something I'm ashamed of? In the closet!

AL: Perfect!

(A door opens and Tonya enters carrying some clothes and shoes. They drop Dick.)

TONYA: Oh! Robin! Hiya, Al.

AL: Hey, Tonya.

(Beat)

TONYA: What're you guys doing?

AL: —Nothing—

ROBIN: —Setting up a sex table for you…

(Beat. Al looks at Robin. Beat.)

AL: Excuse me?

ROBIN: What'd you think? It was for us?

AL: I didn't think about it at all but now that I look at it, it is definitely a sex table.

ROBIN: And thank YOU for HELPING ME set up the sex table.

AL: ANY TIME.

TONYA: You approve of this, Al?

(AL *looks to* ROBIN.)

ROBIN: He does. Enthusiastically. Right, Al?

AL: Yay.

ROBIN: *(Re: the table)* What do you, think?

TONYA: Looks good. Looks real good.

(AL *notices that the lube is lube.*)

AL: Oh, my god—

ROBIN: You're gonna love it, girl!

TONYA: It'll be better than the original plan. Behind the dumpster.

AL: Oh, my god!

TONYA: Robin, I took your advice and got my sexiest outfit. It's an old costume from a play I was in but it'll do the trick.

ROBIN: Everything you do does the trick!

TONYA: Let me help yo—

AL: No!

ROBIN: No! Don't come over here.

AL: Don't!

ROBIN: It's bad luck for the bride to touch the sex table.

AL: Bride?!

TONYA: Bad luck?

ROBIN: Absolutely!

TONYA: That's really a thing?

ROBIN: Definitely! Right, Al?

AL: You shouldn't touch the sex table!

TONYA: Well, I'll take ya'll's word for it.

ROBIN: You run along and get all gussied up. We'll perform the ceremony and then it's straight to Heaven! One way or another.

TONYA: I love you, Robin!

ROBIN: Love you, too, girl!

TONYA: Bye!

ROBIN: Bye sweetie!

(TONYA *exits.*)

ROBIN: Let's get this dead body in the closet.

(AL *and* ROBIN *struggle and can improvise about* DICK *being too limp to stay in, etc. They eventually stand* DICK *up and get him inside the closet but* AL *is inside with him.* ROBIN *notices the bag, grabs it, and closes the door.*)

AL: Ah!

ROBIN: Now, how'd you get in there?

AL: Help... Help.

ROBIN: Ah! Sorry.

(ROBIN *puts the bag on the table and goes back to help* AL. *They stand* DICK *up and get him inside of the closet and the door closed.* AL *starts out.*)

AL: I've gotta find Ruth.

ROBIN: Al! I heard. You're in love with Ruth.

AL: I am.

ROBIN: That's great. What're you gonna tell her about this?

AL: I don't know... (*He starts to exit.*)

ROBIN: Whatever you tell her. Start with "I love you".

AL: Thanks, Robin.

ROBIN: And not "I just killed your husband".

AL: Got it. *(He exits.)*

ROBIN: Al! Hold up a second. We should get our stories straight!

(ROBIN follows AL. As soon as he's gone RUTH enters with the money bag.)

(She checks to make sure no one is there then goes to the closet.)

RUTH: I just can't do it. I can't.

(RUTH almost opens it. She stops short when she sees the bag that ROBIN left out. She goes to it and picks it up.)

RUTH: What the hell is this? *(Then regarding the table)* What the hell is THIS? *(She thinks for a moment, switches the bags, and then leaves in a hurry.)*

(ROBIN enters in a hurry. He starts to wipe for fingerprints. He stops.)

ROBIN: Having killed a man, this sex table and sex toy bag seem kinda weird!

(GRACIE enters with a small bag and a big butcher knife. She's covering her eyes.)

GRACIE: Everybody decent in here?

ROBIN: What do you mean?

GRACIE: Is everybody wearing clothes and… unattached.

ROBIN: Yes…

GRACIE: Ah. You seen Sam?

ROBIN: I haven't.

(GRACIE indicates with the knife and bag.)

GRACIE: I'm making sandwiches. You want one?

ROBIN: No thank you.

GRACIE: Well…you look plum tuckered out. You been working pretty, pretty hard this afternoon haven't you?

ROBIN: Well…as a matter of fact—

GRACIE: Oh! My big O bag!

ROBIN: Your Big what bag?! You know something about this bag?

GRACIE: Sure!

ROBIN: Do you know what's inside this bag?

GRACIE: Sure! Everything in it is mine!

ROBIN: Really?!

GRACIE: Why, yeah! I bring 'em up here after George and I are done with 'em.

ROBIN: Oh. My. God.

GRACIE: Uh, huh. So, other people can enjoy them.

ROBIN: Wh— People here at the church?!

GRACIE: What am I supposed to do, leave them in our bathroom forever?

ROBIN: You keep them in your bathroom?

GRACIE: Uh, huh. George likes to go in there and go to town on them.

ROBIN: Oh, no.

GRACIE: But people here love them, too. I've even seen some of the kids enjoying them.

ROBIN: Gracie, I am shocked!

GRACIE: Oh! YOU'RE shocked!? I figured you wouldn't be so easy to shock, Mr Man.

ROBIN: I'll admit I am an atypical Baptist but…

GRACIE: What do you have against bringing the Big O! into the church?

ROBIN: It's—ah—I… *(Checks the sex table)* …obviously have mixed feelings—I'm not here to—oh, man—not here to judge. Nope. I can't judge.

GRACIE: Well…good. I don't judge you either…for… you know.

ROBIN: What?

GRACIE: You know what I mean…

ROBIN: I don't.

GRACIE: What I saw you doing in here earlier. What you and Al did…to that other feller.

ROBIN: You saw what we did to that man!?

GRACIE: Saw the whole thing! To be honest, I've always suspected you were the type that would do that sorta thing.

ROBIN: You always thought I was capable of…that?

GRACIE: Yup. Ever since that time you got SO mad when the Thompson twins got paint on the curtains in the office—

ROBIN: Well, that was such a fabulous window treatment!

GRACIE: See!

ROBIN: But that doesn't mean that I would…

GRACIE: But you did.

ROBIN: I did.

GRACIE: It was so violent and sloppy.

ROBIN: It was.

GRACIE: You can keep what you've done hidden in the closet or you can let it out for the world to see.

ROBIN: I think we'll keep it in for now.

GRACIE: But I want you to know I don't judge you for it one bit.

ROBIN: You don't?

GRACIE: No way. Heck, I've been around the block. In my youth, I did it a few times myself.

ROBIN: You did?!

GRACIE: Sure! I'd throw a few back, lower my inhibitions, you know? Then I'd go out on the prowl... find a couple of guys and...you know... *(She makes a sticking gesture with the knife accompanied by something vocal on each stab.)*

ROBIN: You did... *(He mimics her vocalizations.)* To two men at once!?

GRACIE: Oh, yeah! One in the front— *(She makes the sticking gestures and noise again.)* And one in the back— *(Again)*

ROBIN: Ahhh!! *(He runs for the exit.)*

GRACIE: Where are you going?!

ROBIN: I'm going to burn this bag! *(He gets mostly out.)*

GRACIE: Robin, you'd better not! *(She's used the knife to point.)*

ROBIN: Ah!

(ROBIN runs out. GRACIE's hot on his heels.)

(TONYA makes a dramatic entrance. She's dressed like Sandra Dee from the end of Grease.)

TONYA: Here I am! I'm all yours baby! Robin can marry us if that's—God, sorry. These sunglasses are very dark— *(She removes them.)* —and there's no one here. *(She puts the glasses back on and runs right into a wall.)* Mother of pearl!

(TONYA fumbles her way out. MARTHA enters from the opposite side.)

MARTHA: HelloI'mhereIloveyouotoo! Shoot. What the—
(She's noticed the table. She goes to it. She admires it and checks the sturdiness in the same way that Robin did earlier. She looks up.) Thank you, Lord.

(MARTHA shimmies out of her dress and gets under the covers. As soon as she disappears from sight, TROY enters, quickly.)

TROY: I'm ready— *(He notices the table and the person under it.)* I'm... Oh, Gosh. *(He walks to the table.)* I'm here...

(MARTHA giggles and wiggles. TROY looks up.)

TROY: This is a very good sign, Lord. Good job. *(To MARTHA)* I— Listen, we don't have to get married first... We can...you know.

(MARTHA giggles. TROY takes off his shirt.)

TROY: Wow, you giggle sexy.

(TROY touches MARTHA and she wiggles and coos. Electricity shoots through him and he's barely able to stay upright.)

TROY: This is exactly how I pictured our first time together. *(He has grabbed what he thinks are her breasts... but they're her elbows.)*

TROY: Mmm...so, that's how they feel...

(MARTHA sticks her head out.)

MARTHA: Honey, those are my elbows!

TROY: AH! *(He flies back across the room!)*

MARTHA: What— What's wrong—

TROY: I— Ah! Ah! *(He stumbles towards a door.)*

MARTHA: Troy! Ravage me, Troy!

TROY: *(Off)* AHH!

(MARTHA *follows him out.* RUTH *enters. Immediately followed by* AL *from the opposite side of the room.*)

AL: Robin! I can't find— *(He sees* RUTH.*)* Ruth.

RUTH: Who can't you find?

AL: Ruth. You—I was looking for you.

RUTH: I was looking for you.

AL: What for?

RUTH: …Nothing. Why were you looking for me?

AL: No reason.

RUTH: Oh…I have something to tell you…

AL: Ah. Are… Are you going to tell me?

RUTH: It's a very hard thing to say…

AL: Like, to pronounce? Is it a medical term?

RUTH: No—

AL: Are you sick!

RUTH: I—I have a secret.

AL: Yeah? I have a secret, too.

RUTH: Oh. What's your secret?

AL: What's yours?

RUTH: I…

AL: Tell me yours, I'll tell you mine.

RUTH: You first.

(Beat)

AL: Let's say them at the same time…

RUTH: Okay…

*(*AL *and* RUTH *silently count.)*

RUTH: I'm in love with you.

AL: I killed your husband.

RUTH: What?!

AL: ...Just kidding. I'm in love with you is what I was going to say.

RUTH: Oh.

AL: I'm in love with you, too.

(Beat)

RUTH: You're in love with me?

AL: I am. And you love me?

RUTH: I do...

AL: Oh.

RUTH: Okay...I have another secret.

AL: Me, too.

(AL and RUTH silently count.)

AL: There is no Rapture.

RUTH: There is no Rapture.

RUTH: Oh...

AL: I have another secret.

RUTH: Me, too...

(AL and RUTH start to count.)

AL: I have three nipp—

RUTH: Wait—how did YOU know there wasn't a rapture?

AL: Uhh... Huh?

(TROY enters and runs across the stage and exits.)

RUTH: How did you kn—

(MARTHA enters.)

MARTHA: You seen Troy?

AL: He went that way.

(MARTHA *exits in a hurry. Never slowing, to* RUTH*:)*

MARTHA: You're hair looks pretty. *(She's gone. Beat)*

RUTH: How did you know that—

*(*TONYA *enters.)*

TONYA: Here I am— *(She pulls her glasses up.)*

TONYA: Crud muffin. Ya'll seen Troy?

RUTH: That way.

TONYA: Thanks! *(She puts her glasses back on and runs to exit and slams into the wall.)* Fart knocker!

(Then TONYA *fumbles, finds the door knob to the wrong door, opens the door, hits the door jam on the way out and finally manages to exit. Beat)*

RUTH: How did—

*(*ROBIN *enters screaming and quickly exits. Beat)*

RUTH: Might as well wait—

*(*GRACIE *enters. She is still after him and waving the knife. She looks at* AL *and* RUTH*.)*

RUTH: That way.

AL: That way.

AL: What were we talking about?

RUTH: The Rapture. How did you know that it wasn't real?

AL: …Science—

RUTH: Are you in on it?

AL: In on it?

RUTH: Are you…with Sam?

AL: How do you mean?

RUTH: He's scamming us… Are you in on it?

AL: …It's not a scam—

RUTH: Oh, my god—

AL: It's just a big lie— It's not what you think—

RUTH: He was stealing!

AL: No way—

RUTH: He was! He was taking all of the money we were giving to the church—

AL: How do you know that?

RUTH: Because I stole it, too! I— Because I stole what he stole… But I brought it back.

AL: Listen…if there was money—to—to borrow Sam had a reason for it—

RUTH: Wait…the bag… It's gone.

AL: What?

RUTH: The money—that I stole from Sam that he stole from us was right there and now it's… Where's Sam?

AL: I don't know—

RUTH: C'mon. He wouldn't leave town without you, would he?

AL: No! We're partners!

RUTH: Oh—you… Oh, Al—

AL: Not partners in crime! Partners in—I can't tell you.

RUTH: Look. I don't care. I just want to get that money back. These people don't deserve to be lied to and they don't deserve to be stolen from!

AL: He didn't steal and he wouldn't leave me…again.

RUTH: He did and…it looks like he has.

AL: You say you love me—just trust me.

RUTH: I can't, Al.

(ROBIN *enters.*)

ROBIN: Help! She's going to kill me!

(GRACIE *enters with the knife.*)

GRACIE: Robin! Why would you incinerate my O! Magazines! Oh! Ruth, Al. Ya'll want a sandwich?

(TROY *enters. He's disheveled but super calm and super cool.*)

TROY: Yo. What's up, everybody?

AL: Troy, did Martha catch up to you?

TROY: Oh, yeah. She caught me all right. Behind the dumpster.

(MARTHA *enters. Disheveled and very pleased.*)

MARTHA: I need a whole pack of cigarettes! I'mma smoke 'em all at once.

RUTH: Has anyone seen Sam?

TROY: Nah.

ROBIN: No.

GRACIE: Nope.

RUTH: Al?

AL: What?

RUTH: Do you know where Sam is?

AL: He's here somewhere—

(ROBIN *notices* SAM'*s clothes.*)

ROBIN: Guys…umm…Sam's clothes…

MARTHA: You know what this means?

GRACIE: Sam is naked somewhere!

MARTHA: No— It means he's been raptured! He left us—

AL: No—

MARTHA: We've been left behind!

TROY: What?!

GRACIE: Why, Lord!?

TROY: It's real.

MARTHA: It was real—

RUTH: It's— It's not—

ROBIN: It's happening!

MARTHA: We're still here!

GRACIE: Oh, no!

AL: —Guys, there's some other explanation—

ROBIN: I knew I'd be left—

TROY: I regret nothing!

AL: No! There's…he wouldn't go without us.

RUTH: He would.

AL: No, he wouldn't! You don't know! He wouldn't go without me!

RUTH: Looks like he did.

AL: He…he wouldn't go without me. He wouldn't. Sam loves me— *(He chokes up.)*

ROBIN: C'mon, Al.

MARTHA: Yeah. We've all been left.

RUTH: Guys, he wasn't raptured—

AL: Ruth! Please… He's gone! What does it matter?! I trusted Sam…

(AL can't continue. Everyone except RUTH goes to comfort him. RUTH goes to another corner to consider the scene.)

MARTHA: We understand, Al. It's okay.

TROY: We all loved Brother Sam.

GRACIE: Best preacher we've ever had.

(Beat)

ROBIN: I understand. But the fact of the matter is God loved Sam. And he hates us and wants us to suffer for a thousand years.

GRACIE: Yeah, that's all.

(*They group hug* AL. *While they do* SAM *enters quietly with the bag. He sees them but not* RUTH. *He almost leaves but sees the other bag. He looks at his bag and back again and decides to risk it. He sneaks into the room. The whole time he is sneaking* RUTH *is following behind him. Right before he switches the bags…*)

RUTH: Hiya, Sam—

SAM: AH!

AL: Sam!

TROY: Brother Sam!

MARTHA: You weren't raptured!

ROBIN: We thought you were raptured!

GRACIE: We thought we was left behind! Like the terrible book series!

MARTHA: The movies were worse!

AL: Sam, I thought you'd ditched me again.

SAM: No way, buddy—

RUTH: Where have you been?

SAM: …The lord told me to venture forth.

RUTH: Why did you take half your clothes off?

MARTHA: Yeah?

AL: I got you that shirt for my birthday.

SAM: The Lord told me to. (*To* AL) It's just a shirt, buddy.

RUTH: The Lord tell you to ditch your partner and skip town?

AL: It was J Crew.

SAM: Ummm…no. *(To* AL*)* Factory… It was J Crew Factory.

MARTHA: What's going on?

RUTH: Brother Sam…I'm sorry, Al. Sam is…

AL: Please…

RUTH: I'm so sorry, Al. Sam's been skimming our tithe for the last year and he plans to use this fake Rapture to disappear!

(Beat)

SAM: Nuh-uh.

AL: That is—I'm sorry, that is just not true!

RUTH: Al—

AL: No, Ruth! Look—I—I love you Ruth. I love you. I love you! I'm in love with you! I love everything about you except that you keep saying this. It's not—

RUTH: It's true—

AL: —It's not. I'm sorry, it's not!

RUTH: He asked us to give more—

MARTHA: Twenty percent—

RUTH: But it's not all going in to the bank. I did the math. Real math.

GRACIE: Is that true, Sam?

SAM: Brothers and Sisters…I am your preacher. I am a man of God. He chose to speak to me. When I got here you people needed to be healed. So, I healed you. And you looked at the world outside of these walls and wanted to escape it, so I provided you an escape. Who are you going to believe. Me? Or the part-time accountant?

MARTHA: Ruth is the most honest, salt of the earth person I've ever met. And I've known her since she was twelve.

TROY: I've known her since I was a baby.

GRACIE: I knew her momma when her momma was a baby.

ROBIN: We've known you a year and Ruth is like family. I believe in Ruth.

(SAM *runs and they all chase him.*)

(*All of their watch and phone alarms go off at the same time. They all stop and look up expectantly. Nothing happens. They turn them off and look at* SAM.)

(*Beat.* SAM *runs again and everyone chases him, blocking him from every door.*)

(TROY *grabs him.*)

TROY: Gotcha!

(SAM *puts his hand on* TROY's *head and shouts—*)

SAM: Be healed!

(TROY *flies backwards.* SAM *turns and heals* MARTHA.)

SAM: Demons out!

(MARTHA *flies backwards.*)

MARTHA: He got away! My tennis elbow feels great, though!

AL: No! Please! Everybody. You don't know him— the way I know him! Nobody was stealing money! I promise! Sam loves you! He—Sam, I have to tell them what we do together—

SAM: No, Al—

AL: I have to—

SAM: They won't understand—

RUTH: You were a part of it, I knew it!

AL: I was! I am—

RUTH: Oh, Al—

AL: This man has given so much, not just to you—but to mankind—

ROBIN: What are you talking about?

SAM: Al—

AL: He's not a preacher—

MARTHA: We know that now—

AL: He's more than that! He's a doctor. He's a scientist.

SAM: No, Al—

AL: He has an I Q of 267! His real name is Dr Samuel Beckett! And—and he travels around…leaping…from one life to the next, setting things right that once went wrong!

SAM: Ohh, boy…

ROBIN: That sounds familiar—

RUTH: He's a conman—

AL: No! I'd know if he was. I'm his partner—

SAM: Sidekick—

AL: —I'm his sidekick partner.

SAM: Just—just sidekick, buddy.

AL: —I'm his sidekick and he loves me.

RUTH: Then he has you fooled, too.

AL: I believe in him! I have faith in my friend—here— (*He grabs the bag from* SAM.) Let me show you—

SAM: No—

AL: This is a testament!

SAM: —Al—

AL: —Here's what he's here to do for you!

(AL *opens the bag dramatically and empties its contents. Sex toys spill out of the bag onto the floor. There is a silence as a Rabbit vibrates its way around the floor.*)

(*Beat*)

MARTHA: Hallelujah.

(*The closet door opens and DICK emerges. His forehead is bloody from the wicker basket that ROBIN put on his head. His pony tail is out so his long hair, his beard, the sheet he's wrapped in, the bloody wound in his side, his bloody outstretched hands, the backlighting from the closet, and the angelic sounds of the choir make it seem as if Jesus has entered the room. Everyone exclaims.*)

GRACIE: He is risen!!

TROY: He is risen, indeed!

DICK: Ruth, I've come for you—

MARTHA: I knew she'd be first—

(*RUTH acts fast. She grabs a big purple dildo off of the floor and attacks DICK with it.*)

RUTH: DICK!!

(*RUTH knocks DICK out with one mighty blow and bat flips.*)

MARTHA: Ruth!!!

TROY: Ruth! You are going to Hell!!!

RUTH: What?!?

GRACIE: Jesus came out of the closet, you called him a Dick and knocked the hell outta him with a extra large Dildo!

MARTHA: That was the medium.

(*TONYA makes her dramatic entrance. She delivers the whole speech to GRACIE.*)

TONYA: Here I am! I'm all yours baby! Robin can marry us if that's what you want! I'll do that to make you happy but first you've gotta know something about me...I love my body! I love pleasure! In Junior High, one day I climbed a pole on our playground and slid slowly down it and holy f-ing guacamole! After that day I would wolf down my lunch and rush outside so I could climb that pole and slide down it! Climb up it! Slide down it! All recess long! Five days a week! The teachers thought I was autistic! Later that summer I discovered I could make myself feel that way! And then my senior year I found out boys could make me feel that way! And when I got to community college, a couple of girls! And a couple more! The point is...I'm not a virgin. Not even close. And I'm sorry if that makes you feel different about me but I am who I am— At this point in my life I'm super sexual and pansexual and screw my mom for calling me a slut just because she has a stick up her butt and not in a fun way! I say what I want AND what I don't want and as I get older I'm getting cooler and weirder and I feel myself morphing into like a female Matthew McConaughey, confusing but sexy and I love it I love it I love it I love it I love it I love it I love it I love it I love it! I've been with who I wanted, when I wanted and right now I only want to be with you in our last moments on this Earth! What do ya say?

GRACIE: Oh, hell, why not?

(TONYA *takes off her glasses and sees she's talking to* GRACIE.)

TONYA: Ah! (*She notices that everyone is there.*) Ah! (*She notices* DICK.) Ah! Who killed Jesus?

RUTH: It's not Jesus. It's my husband, Dick.

MARTHA: Dick!?

ROBIN: Dick.

RUTH: Dick.

AL: Dick.

MARTHA: That Dick looks like Jesus.

GRACIE: So, does George's…after the accident. People came from all over to see—

RUTH: —Not now, Gracie.

AL: Dick tried to kill me and Robin earlier.

ROBIN: But we killed him first.

RUTH: You did!?

AL: Yeah. Sorta.

RUTH: You guys got the best of Dick?

ROBIN: Apparently, we are very strong and brutal men.

AL: Yeah, we're pretty brutal.

RUTH: I have a confession…Dick is…my doorknob…

(Beat. RUTH *points to her eye. They all get it. Oh!)*

RUTH: I knew that Sam was stealing. And Dick found out. He was trying to get me to steal the money, too… But I…I did. I'm sorry. I stole it and was going to use it to leave him… But I brought it back and left it here on this…is this a sex table?

ROBIN: YOU left it here?

RUTH: Yeah…

ROBIN: I hid it in the baptismal from Gracie because she was trying to kill me—

GRACIE: What?!

ROBIN: *(Scared)* I mean… Ha! Kidding. She's just a… sweet idiosyncratic old lady…and not capable of such a thing…

GRACIE: That's right.

AL: I trusted you, Sam!

SAM: Now, Al, hold on—

AL: No! No more holding on. "Hold on" is what you told me when I was in that Mexican prison for a month!

SAM: But—

AL: I know what you're going to say. And, yes, that is where I met Javier. And, yes, he is now one of my three best pen pals, so I have no regrets. But what about Nepal?!

SAM: I knew you were going to bring up Nepal.

AL: Of course, I'm going to bring up Nepal! Those goats were endangered!

SAM: But I didn't leave without you—

AL: Only because I befriended the seaplane pilot—

SAM: We both made friends with...

AL: What was his name?

SAM: Baloo?

AL: I can't believe I have followed you this long! I can't cover for you this time.

SAM: You're right. You are absolutely right, Al. I was wrong, and you should turn me in.

AL: I will turn you in!

SAM: Oh. I didn't expect you to say that. I'm sorry. I like each and every one of you but I am who I am. I thought, "Perfect! A conman in a place that demands unquestioning faith!" I mean my whole life has been about easing skepticism without raising curiosity. Then I officiated your weddings and your funerals and... Anyway. I'm sorry.

GRACIE: How did you heal my glaucoma?

SAM: I healed you at the hospital after your glaucoma surgery.

GRACIE: Riiiggght.

RUTH: Someone needs to tell everyone else the Rapture isn't real.

TONYA: There's no rapture?

ROBIN: No, darlin', it was a scam.

TONYA: Yes! I was so worried it was real!!

ROBIN: What?

TONYA: I've been freaking out for no reason! I was NOT ready for judgement day. Were ya'll?

(There's a beat and a general "No".)

TONYA: I mean I at least want to finish this semester.

AL: Somebody has to break all of this to the congregation.

GRACIE: I reckon I should be the one to tell them.

AL: Be gentle with them, Gracie.

GRACIE: Oh, I've been breaking bad news ever since George's first colonoscopy. *(She opens the door—)* That's it! Rapture's off!! Let's get the hell outta here!

(There's a cheer. GRACIE's gone. ROBIN has found some fuzzy handcuffs and puts them on SAM.)

ROBIN: Now, Ruth, about your husband…if we— *(Re: him and AL.)* —if we …dicks have offended, think but this, and all is mended-—

RUTH: If you're apologizing for trying to kill my husband, don't bother. You know, sometimes when people keep…running into a doorknob, they start looking for another door to go out of. *(She crosses to stand over DICK.)* When what they should have been doing is getting rid of that doorknob.

(ROBIN *indicates to* AL.)

ROBIN: Or maybe...replace that doorknob with another, sweeter one?

AL: Ruth, Robin is right. I want to help you with your doorknob situation. I mean, I'll be honest, I'm not very handy with tools or anything, but surely someone in the church—

RUTH: Al...I liked the idea of the rapture at first. I think it was my chance to run away from my problems. Then when I put two and two together, figured out what Sam was up to... It was still my chance to run...I've been hurt, Al—

AL: I know.

RUTH: And I'm sick of being hurt—

AL: I know.

RUTH: I won't be hurt again. Not by you, not by anyone.

AL: I know.

RUTH: I won't let it happen.

AL: Ruth, I've travelled the world with Sam. And I've been a lot of things I couldn't have ever been on my own. A weather man, a fish handler for a trained seal, a blind golf caddy, a really bad dentist... But I've never been in love. Not until now.

EVERYONE: Awwwe.

RUTH: I've heard all of that so many times. And every time...every time, Al—I always wanted to believe. Now, I don't know if I can.

(*Disappointed "Awwwe"*)

AL: Well... That's okay. But I believe in you, Ruth.

(*A sweet "Awwwe"*)

RUTH: Al, you believe in everything.

(*Everyone is disappointed again.*)

SAM: If I could… (*Steps over* DICK's *body to stand between* RUTH *and* AL) You're right, Ruth. Al…he believes in everything. And I do mean everything. It's pathological. He believed me when I told him that Zima was bottled from the fountain of youth.

(AL *is shocked.*)

AL: Then that means I'm—

SAM: Forty-one years old.

(AL *gasps!*)

RUTH: Is there a point to any of this?

SAM: This man…this sweet ticklish man. He has blindly put his faith in so many things over the years. He believes in more than anyone I have ever met. And let me tell you, I've met some real dumb suckers in my day.

AL: Thanks, Sam!

SAM: Sure thing, buddy. I don't deserve him. But the two of you…Al is a true believer…and, well, you're just true, Ruth. I've been witness to this man's faith for years now. And you're the first thing I've seen worthy of it.

(*Everybody "Awwwes".*)

RUTH: You'll have to earn me. Starting now.

AL: I'll do my best.

(*"Awwwe". Beat.* RUTH *kisses* AL. *Everyone cheers!* SAM *has slipped out in the commotion.*)

MARTHA: Where's Sam?

(*They all notice* SAM's *gone.*)

AL: He Quantum Leaped!

(Blackout. The play could end there if you choose. You can also do the following.)

Epilogue

(Lights up on a small keyboard. GRACIE *enters and talks to the audience. While she talks she sits at a keyboard and gets some sheet music ready.)*

GRACIE: Oh! Nice turn out for the wedding! It'll be starting in a minute. Oh, my…you have chosen to wear jeans to the wedding…that's nice. Bless your heart. Listen, this side over here is friends of the groom. And this side is friends of the bride. So, if you're on the wrong side now's the time to switcheroo… No? okay.

*(*AL *enters.)*

GRACIE: You nervous?

AL: I can't stop shaking.

GRACIE: The first wedding is the hardest.

AL: How's George?

GRACIE: You won't believe it but I was feeling puny last week and that man waited on me hand and foot.

AL: That's nice.

GRACIE: It was nice. And I abused the privilege like a middle aged white man.

Troy enters.

TROY: Al! Nervous?

AL: I think I'm gonna throw up.

TROY: Please don't.

*(*RUTH *enters.)*

AL: Ruth!

RUTH: Al! *(She kisses him.)* Nervous?

TROY: He thinks he's going to throw up.

RUTH: Please don't.

AL: I'll try not to. Hey! I heard from Sam.

RUTH: Yeah?

AL: I think he's finally gone straight. I got a letter from him. Says he got a job at Goldman Sachs.

(The recessional starts. ROBIN and TONYA enter together. ROBIN stands next to TROY and TONYA peels off to the other side. Let's somehow get the entire audience to rise. Everyone is at attention as MARTHA enters. She's glowing and nine months pregnant. She arrives and everyone settles. TROY settles across from her.)

MARTHA: Brother Al— Can— Sorry, I just wanted to let everyone know I'm dilated to about a foot and a half so we're going to need to speed this sucker up.

AL: Okay! Um— We're gathered here to join these… um, then my speech, I'll boil it down—honor… Oh! Forgive your partner— Forgive…um…I think maybe the most important thing in life is to know who YOU are, and to be okay with it. Cherish yourself, too. No matter what.

(To the closest guy in the audience.)

ROBIN: See Clark! Best preacher we've ever had!

(ROBIN blows him a kiss and indicates to the room "That's him." Everyone is impressed.)

AL: The couple wrote their own vows—

(TROY reads his vows.)

TROY: Martha, I can't believe you're gonna be my old lady. You used to just be a old lady.

MARTHA: What the f—

(AL puts his hand on MARTHA.)

AL: ...forgive...

TROY: Ha. Ha. I thought that was funny, too. All my life I've felt like I had an angel on one shoulder and a devil on the other. And they both kept telling me what I should want or not want. But when I met you...it's like...there was another voice...one that just...stood straight up in the middle of them.

MARTHA: Straight as an arrow.

TROY: Uh huh—

MARTHA: With a little upward angle to it...

TROY: Those voices on my shoulder? They're not angels and devils—they're other people's voices. And they been nagging at me all my life. But that big, throbbing voice in the middle? That's mine.

MARTHA: And what's yours is mine, baby.

TROY: And it wants to know what I want. And what I want is you, Martha.

EVERYBODY: Awwwe.

AL: Okay...a little more double entendre than I anticipated, but—

MARTHA: Oh, baby!

AL: Yep. Okay.

MARTHA: Baby, I love you. You and me and everyone here today—we've all been looking our whole lives for something true to stick our faith in. And when you're that desperate, believe me, you'll stick it in just about anything. And once you've stuck it in enough wrong places, you're in danger of it getting diseased and falling off. Start to wonder if there's any point in having it at all. But there is. I know there is. We all deserve to believe in something. We all deserve to feel it given back to us. You restored my faith in love, Troy.

(Everyone "Awwwe")

*(*MARTHA*'s water breaks all over the floor. Everyone "Ewwww".)*

(Black out)

END OF PLAY